T0197520

A Woman's Search *for the* Heart *of* God!

THE TRUE STORY OF TRISH VERNON'S AMAZING JOURNEY FOR THE RIGHTEOUSNESS OF GOD AND HIS KINGDOM

NYLE T. VERNON

WestBow Press books may be ordered through booksellers or by contacting:

WestBow Press
A Division of Thomas Nelson & Zondervan
1663 Liberty Drive
Bloomington, IN 47403
www.westbowpress.com
844.714.3454

Scripture taken from the King James Version of the Bible.

ISBN: 978-1-6642-0275-7 (sc)
ISBN: 978-1-6642-0276-4 (e)

Library of Congress Control Number: 2020916005

Print information available on the last page.

WestBow Press rev. date: 08/31/2020

WESTBOW
PRESS®
A DIVISION OF THOMAS NELSON
& ZONDERVAN

Foreword

I consider it a great honor to share the journals written by my late wife of 53 years, Patricia Peak Vernon. She was truly a chosen vessel of the Lord! Her life, her dreams, and her prayers were all centered around God. As the years began to roll by, it seemed to only intensify her desire to worship God in ways I could hardly imagine. Her day by day diary will speak volumes as she describes in detail her commitment.

The awesome miracles she experiences will astonish you as you feel the Holy Spirit responding to her worship. In 2001, God moved in a very strange way as He was about to call us into full-time ministry. But first, He showed us His Power. One night in 2001, I awakened to find her lying on the bedroom floor at 3:13 a.m. with no sign of life in her body; no pulse, no heartbeat, no breath. She was cold and stiff. Her eyes were open, fixed, and glazed. She had died! In desperation, I began to call on God to return her life to her body. Praying for about 35 minutes, I looked down and her little finger began to move! In just minutes, she sat up and said, "Where are the angels?" GOD HAD DECIDED TO LET HER LIVE!!! As you read this book, I pray that you will begin to seek the righteousness of God and His Glory!

Dedication

I would like to dedicate this book to the following people who helped shape our lives over the years.

To Trish's family...I love you all so much
To my Dad, Horace Edward Vernon
To my Mom, Virginia Mae Vernon
To my Grandfather, W.M. Lowman
To my Grandmother, Bertha Vashti Lowman
To my uncles, Elroy and Dudley Lowman
To a great man of God, C.T. Davidson
To our mentors, Malcolm and Hannah Linkous
To our former Pastor and his wife, Tim and Kelly Coalter
To our best friends, Larry and Frankie Dotson
And to hundreds of others who prayerfully supported us.

Part I

The Life And Times Of Patricia P. Vernon And How God Guided Her Life...

1949-2018

This book was written from her journals in her own words and is dedicated to her memory. To God by the glory!

Trish with her sister Brenda in 1953 on Easter Sunday

There is much to be said about the life of Trish, but I want to begin at the age of nine. One day there came a knock at the front door. Trish arrived first and opened the door to welcome the visitors. "Little girl," said one of the women, "we are visiting in the neighborhood inviting newcomers to our little Baptist church just down the road and were wondering if you attend church anywhere?" Trish replied, "No ma'am. I sure would like to, but my parents won't take me." One of the women said, "Why don't you ask them if we could come by at 10:00 and pick you up and bring you back at 1:00. Would they let you go?"

Sure enough, Trish was able to get permission to go to church for the very first time. The first Sunday she attended, the pastor spoke about a place called heaven and how God sent His only Son, Jesus, to the world so that the world could be saved. All you had to do was ask forgiveness for your sins and accept Him into your heart. She accepted Jesus on that very first Sunday morning at that little Baptist Church!

By the next Sunday morning, she was hungry to learn more. The pastor spoke about the Bible as the true Word of God! It was then Trish realized that her family did not even own a Bible except a very large family type that was used to record births and deaths. Why, it was way too big to carry around. She desperately wanted her very own personal Bible.

The following Sunday, the pastor announced they were going to have an attendance contest beginning the next week. The person who invited and brought the most people to church within 30 days would win............. A BRAND NEW, RED LETTER EDITION, KING JAMES PERSONAL BIBLE! Trish's heart began to yearn to own that bible as her very own!

She began to knock on every door in her neighborhood inviting people to church. She went to school and began to invite students and teachers alike. No one had ever seen such enthusiasm! Many of her contacts came just out of curiosity. Finally, her pastor announced that they had a winner of the prize. Guess who? Patricia Peak! She told me later that this was the most valuable gift she had ever received. When we got married many years later, she still had that red leather Bible.

My background was slightly different than Trish's. Whereas she came from a family who never served God, she was the very first on in her family to bring the "light of the gospel" into that home of four siblings and two parents. Later on, every one of her brothers and sisters and her mother accepted Jesus Christ as their Savior!! What a joy that God had chosen to use a nine-year old girl to be the first to share the gospel.

On the other hand, I had been raised in a Pentecostal church since my birth in 1944. There were many ministers in my family including my grandfather, W.M. Lowman, and my father, H.E. Vernon. As a result, we were taught that God has many blessings other than salvation. We believed in a Holy Spirit filled life.

This was all new to my wife, Trish, as she began to attend the church where my father pastored. After about two months, she received the Holy Spirit during a revival which began her desire to seek for the deeper things of God. As the years passed, Trish never missed church even though it meant having to dress our three small children. Even during a time of revival, which sometimes lasted three weeks, they were in attendance. She told me later that was why all three children were serving God today. They sat in church and listened to the Word. She encouraged them to read and study the Bible at an early age!

Many miracles of healing occurred in her life and I will share some of them in this book. Many were led to Christ during the next several years. In the year of 2018 on Mother's Day, God took her home after 20 additional years he granted her. We had an awesome miracle to happen in the year 2000 which would change our lives forever. Perhaps, someone who is reading this book right now, will receive your healing or calling into the ministry.

This is Trish's true story you are about to read. It all began in the year 2000 as her obsession with finding more about God's righteousness began to deepen. She went into a two-year time of daily intercessory prayer which changed her life forever. Her hunger for studying out every word in the scriptures became her daily bread. One way she was able to communicate with God was to write down everything she felt in her spirit in a journal. To my knowledge, no one had ever read what she had written until after her death when we discovered them. For many years, we had searched for those journals but to no avail. Two weeks after her passing, we found them between her recipe books! Maybe it was the will of God to tell her story of seeking God to someone who is reading this book right now! I feel it is time to share what God had given to her during her two-year incredible journey.

She had kept a day-to-day diary as we traveled throughout the Southeastern United States in my career. She would sit in the car and begin to worship the Lord while I called on my clients. As God would reveal the scriptures to her, a note would be recorded in her diary and then added to her journals. Little did she know what God had planned in her life because of her seeking.

What you are reading at this point will be the very words of Trish as recorded in her journals. Nothing has been changed or edited.

My Personal Testimony

Around the latter part of December, I began to seek for more of God's Spirit in my life. I began to pray more and listen to His Word in different ways. Having purchased some of Joyce Meyers tapes and what a "real plus" in my life that was! These tapes blessed me because they told me about my weaknesses and what to do about them. But I also watched Christian television and was so blessed by God's Presence.

One day in January, Nyle was out of town and I was home alone feeling devastated by the separation of my daughter's seventeen-year marriage. I knew to pray and that God would help me, but I was overwhelmed! In the bed one night for several hours of sleeplessness, I cried out to God, "O God! Are you even aware? I need to know! Please show me that you care about what we are going though! Give me a sign that you hear and love me!"

Finally, I went to sleep. The next day, the 18th of January, I got up and began Bible study. God was teaching me to study more, pray more, and to search Him out. God was putting such a desire in my heart for me to seek Him. Troy and Kathy (my son and daughter-in-law), had given me a series of tapes for Christmas and I thought I would listen to them today. So I took the tapes and went to my van and drove around just listening to them. I had planned to just listen to a couple of tapes today and maybe a couple more tomorrow. Suddenly, I realized it was 5:00 p.m. I had become so involved in the teaching on the tapes, I had rode around almost all day! I was so blessed! There were two of them on worshipping God that grasped my soul and changed my life.

Private Testimony-God gave me an insight on worship to Him and how He moves and answers prayer through worship from your heart just because you recognize who He is! Worshipping, not worrying, about everything and trying to figure out the answers, but knowing He is in control and leaving all our provision and needs up to Him. I worshipped Him all day on January 18th and prayed much and worshipped and prayed and worshipped again. Praise God!

On the 19th of January, I was on the phone to Renee, my daughter after my devotions and began to share them with her. I usually have my glasses hanging over the collar of my blouse when I need to read. Renee and I were talking when I looked down and told Renee, "This is strange! This has never happened before but there is a layer of frosty-like dust on my glasses." It's not like I have been cleaning or dusting as I had just finished my devotions. Oh well! I'll just clean them again.

After I had hung up the phone, I went into my powder room and looked into the mirror. "What in the world is this?" It looked like little particles of dust in my hair! Well, I just started trying to brush them out, but each time, it just came back about three or four times!

Nyle had come in wondering what was going on. When I explained to him about these little particles that had fallen upon me, he got a little cup and began to pick little particles of gold that had fallen to the floor; maybe twenty or thirty pieces and set them on the window ledge. The next morning they had all disappeared! We were in amazement at this miracle from heaven!

Later that evening, Nyle returned home and after dinner, we began to retire for bed. Normally I sit at my vanity bench and primp and dental floss. But on this night, when I sat down, I noticed something and called Nyle to come and see! On the lower left side of my mouth were three fillings shining in my mouth like gold! Sparkling gold! What is this? "Nyle, what do you see?" He said, "Trish, it looks like gold!" Now you must understand I have never been to a dentist or anywhere else and got gold fillings in my mouth! Matter-of-fact, the fillings that were put there in 1994 had been dark, almost the color of lead.

Now, Nyle and I can't see that well anymore, so we did not know what to think! Finally, we settled down and went to bed. I did not sleep much thinking about the gold teeth in my mouth! The first thing the next morning, I jumped out of bed and ran and grabbed a flashlight and my glasses. Opening my mouth as wide as I could in front of the mirror, sure enough, there were three gold fillings, bright and shining! I ran downstairs to Nyle's office and yelled, "Look at the gold teeth!"

We began to laugh and laugh in the spirit of the Lord thanking Him for the miracle we had witnessed. Why? I'm not real sure but I asked God for a sign. Just a few months before, I had spoken to several people about gold dust falling from heaven and things like that. It was confirmed that indeed God had performed this miracle on several occasions and I remembered saying, "I want that to happen to me!" I just simply believe in God's signs and wonders. It all came together now as to what happened on January nineteenth. God visited me as the gold dust fell from heaven! Thank you, Father!

This was an awesome miracle that I held very precious to my heart. God's supernatural miracles are still real today. He is the same, yesterday, today, and forever! Just like when He parted the Red Sea, turned the water into wine, fed the five thousand with a two-piece fish dinner, saved Daniel from the hungry lion, brought the three Hebrew boys out of a fiery furnace, caused the large fish to swallow up Jonah, and on and on!

As God had given me the gift of the Holy Ghost with the evidence of speaking in tongues, I had never had the gift to interpret the heavenly language. Shortly after the miracle of the gold dust, that would change. One day while worshipping God in what felt like heaven on earth, God began to speak a message in tongues. After the message was given, I began to understand the words! Here are the exact words as I had written them down.

"FEAR NOT, BE NOT AFRAID. MY POWER IS GREATER THAN ANY POWER SATAN COULD EVER HAVE! I AM WITH YOU AND WILL ANOINT YOU! I HAVE ENCAMPED AROUND YOUR DWELLING PLACE, YOUR HOME, A PLACE OF ANGELS!"

Nyle was gone at the time, but when he returned that evening, I was still shaking from my encounter with God as His Glory was still on me. His presence was so powerful I actually had to lay my body down lying only face-down on the sofa crying and weeping before the Lord! When we worship and pray daily, our house will become a "house of prayer!" This will cause us to lead our church into a "house of prayer." Folks, the time is now! We do not have to keep waiting, knowing something is coming…IT IS HERE!

Open yourself up to God's calling and receive the supernatural move of Him! There are anointed ones in our congregations that God wants to use! You have been held back concerned about what someone will think. A real move of God will change things in your home! A real move of God will bring miracles! God wants us to worship Him not only in our churches but in our homes!

When we sold our home in Virginia to go into full-time ministry, the buyers told us "When we came through the front doors, we felt a very peaceful feeling, almost as if angels were living here!" Praise the Lord!

The home we lived in at the time of Trish's miracle of the "gold dust." After that encounter, it seemed to be full of angels until the day we moved to Florida to begin our full-time ministry.

God has shown me so much of His Spirit that I crave more of Him; like craving food. We must seek Him daily and learn to pray the way He teaches us. We have made prayer so difficult and wasted so much time trying to seek Him, we have missed out on His presence. I am looking for a greater move of God! In the past, I have experienced in my time of worship and prayer, that His presence was so great, that it literally overwhelmed me!

Tuesday, March 21, 2000

Nyle and I left out early this morning towards Tennessee, traveling in his job. I wasn't feeling very well today; was up most of the night with my stomach hurting. But I feel somewhat better now. Praise the Lord! I am getting ready to study God's Word that He wants to feed to me today. Lord give me what you wish to teach me that I might be anointed to do something for you on this day! My desire today is great for more of Him in my life; I just want to worship Him so much! God is so good! (My walk). Isaiah 43:1, "Fear not, for I have redeemed you. I have summoned you by name. You are mine." (These are the words God gave me for today.) Philippians 1:6, "Being confident of this very thing that he which hath begun a good work in you will perform it until the day of Jesus Christ." Thank you, Lord! Romans 8:30-39, "God has justified us as we will be more than conquerors because we can never be in life separated from God!" The Spirit assures of future glory and the Spirit assures us of final victory! Thank you, God for my Bible study time today. It has truly lifted my spirit and assured me that you are with me and have a work for me. I desire your anointing! I feel God's presence so powerfully with me right this moment. I love you Father. Teach me, teach me, teach me your ways! Guide me into your paths! Hallelujah!

Psalm 63:1-5, Praise releases blessings and satisfaction. I just want to thank you God, for Your Word today. I needed the assurance that your hand is leading me; and I will wait on Your guidance into service.

Wednesday, March 22, 2000

Well, its time; Pastor Coalter wants me to share my supernatural miracle with the congregation. God has prompted my heart, so I am making myself willing and to bless others. Our message from our pastor this past Sunday was to let your blessings from God flow through a funnel and not to just have a full cup for just you alone. That was truly my confirmation! You may say, why do you hesitate? Because of the supernatural evidence of this. I want people to receive it from God, not as a show. We must be ready to accept the bad with the good.

"Lord, I am asking for your help and anointing because this is for your glory. And I thank you for pouring into my vessel."

Today's study-Colossians 1:9, "For this reason, since the day we heard about you, we have not stopped praying for you and asking God to fill you with the knowledge of His will through all spiritual wisdom and understanding." Thank you Jesus.

Nyle and I are still on the road. Thank you Father for allowing me to travel with my husband. It's a lovely day and God is good! My mind has been traveling from person to person to pray for. Peggy Speed for one. God bless her this moment. My daughter Renee called and said they took Trevor to the doctor with strep throat and infected ears. God be his Jehovah Rophe, his healer this moment! Praise God.

"Father, I am trying to change my weakness into strengths; but I'm still having some thoughts of fear now and then. At the times this happens, I turn my thoughts more to You and begin worshipping You! Sometimes there does not seem to be a way that things could work out, but I fully trust You because I know Your Word is true. This is not a fairly-tale; it's a true story and Your promises are true! If we obey, pray, worship and live the way you teach us, your promises belong to us and that promises us to be blessed! Glory to God! I love you Lord. You are my life and my everything. I am nothing, nothing, nothing without You."

Father, you are my Jehovah.
Jehovah Tsidkenu-You are the Lord of my righteousness.
Jehovah M'kaddesh- You are my sanctifier.
Jehovah Shalom-You are my peace.
Soundness-The Keeper of my mind, soul and body.
Success-The Lord's provision shall be seen.
Nissi-My banner
Rohi-My Shepherd
The Lord that gives me victory and leads and guides in all things.

3-23-2000
The language of love. Verse for today. Luke 13:16, "And ought not this woman being a daughter of Abraham who Sarah hath bound, lo, these eighteen years, be loosed from this bond on Sabbath Day?"

3-27-00
Time for devotions. God feed me Your Word and teach me this day.
2 Corinthians 4:16, "For which cause we faint not; but though our outward man perish; yet the inward man is renewed day by day."

Even on a bad day, just keep talking to God! 2 Corinthians 4:18, "While we look not on the things which are seen, but at the things which are not seen; for the things which are seen are temporal; but the things which are not seen are eternal."

3-30-00
Verse for today in devotions. Psalms 19:1, "The heavens declare the glory of God; and the firmament shows His handiwork." Jesus, this day, let our actions and attitudes be in sync with all creation. May we articulate praise with the moments we are given today and every day! Amen.

"Praise you Lord! I will praise you. I'll say that I love you in a thousand ways! Hallelujah!" Other scriptures for study; Proverbs 4:23-27, Matthew 5:14-16. Protect your mind and thoughts. Let your light so shine as to glorify God. Have a positive effect on people. Live responsibly to glorify God.

"Heavenly Father, help me to let your glory filter through my life to draw others to you." I want to think and meditate on Godly words and actions. Anoint me with your fire!"

The Armor of God
Helmet of Salvation
Breastplate of Righteousness
Shield of Faith
Sword of the Spirit
Belt of Truth
Lord, shod my feet with the gospel of peace

4-4-20
James 5:13-20 Scripture of the day.
"Women of Prayer"
It is time for us women to "spiritually grow-up." There have been women of prayer that have gone to be with the Lord such as Agnes Sanford, Corrie Ten Boom, Catherine Marshall, as well as women that we know personally that prayed for the world! Unless we begin to grow up spiritually, unless we become convinced that we are the generation of Christian adults ultimately responsible for the spiritual condition of our nation, there could be a void of this type of God-Seekers!

We must know and understand that there are few left in the generation ahead to pray for this world. We are coming of age, but are coming to terms with our lack of spiritual depth and ability. It is us who must learn the meaning of "forbearing". It is us who must develop the discipline of spiritual perseverance, not shrinking back from growth but doing the will of God, having our faith and keeping our soul. It is we who must become women of faith and prayer and obedience and service! It is we who must set a spiritual standard for the next generation. It is time for us all to grow up for prayer.

4-6-00

Scripture reading- Ephesians 3:16-20

"Strengthened with might" is to literally become mighty by His Power, which the Holy Spirit brings to work in the believer. Verse 3:17, Rooted like a tree and grounded like a building on a strong foundation. Verse 3:18, Comprehend means to receive expeditionary insight and not to simply understand intellectually. Verse 19, To know the love of Christ is the essence of the greatest fullness. All the fullness of God speaks of more than one experience or more than one aspect of His truth and power. It points to a broad-based spirituality, balances through participating in all of God's blessings, resources and wisdom! Verse 3:20, Now unto Him that is able to do exceeding abundantly above all that we ask or think according to the power that worketh in us.

A word from God today: find a secret place for refuge. Under His wings shall you trust and find refuge. Psalm 91:4. But when we start seeking answers to all the problems and situations that confront us, trying to fulfill our desire rather than God's will, we get out from under the shadow of His wings. Seek the Kingdom of God! With the benefits the desire to praise and worship will be present. Do you realize that you don't even have to worry about your own spiritual growth? All you need to do is seek the Kingdom, meaning the Spirit as in heaven and you will grow! Seek God, abide in Him and He will cause increase and growth. A baby just drinks milk and grows. All you and I have to do is to desire the sincere milk of the Word and you will grow. 1 Peter 2:2 We can never experience any real measure of success by our own human effort. Instead we must seek first the Kingdom of God and His righteousness, then all these other things we need will be added to us. We are not to seek God's presents (such as gifts), but His presence! Let us desire to seek, inquire for, and insistently require that we dwell in the house of the Lord in His presence all the days of our life to behold and gaze upon the beauty, the sweet attractiveness and the delightful loveliness of the Lord. Meditate, consider and inquire in His Temple for in the day of trouble He will hide us in His shelter; in the secret of His tent will He hide us. He will set us high upon a rock and now shall my head be lifted up above my enemies round about me! I will offer sacrifices and shouting of joy. I will sing, yes, I will sing praise to the Lord. Psalm 27:3-6

When we seek Him and His Kingdom, we begin to desire more of Him causing a desire of worship and praise. Philippians 4:6, "Be careful for nothing; but in everything by prayer and supplication with thanksgiving let your requests be made known to God."

TESTIMONY OF A HEALING MIRACLE!

May, 2006

Our church in Oviedo felt a need that Trish and I needed a little vacation and that we loved the beach. So they raised funds and presented us with a reservation coupon to an ocean-front hotel at Daytona Beach! We were thrilled. So the following week, off to the mini-vacation we went for a three day break. Arriving at the hotel, we found the only parking place that was only two spaces down from the dumpster. Oh well it would work even though someone had placed a concrete curb bumper at the wrong end of the space. Never the less, we began to unload the car. Trish grabbed a small suitcase and backed up a couple of steps only to fall backwards over the concrete curb bumper. I ran over to assist her only to find that she had broken her wrist. Helping her up, I said, "Trish, we need to take you to the emergency room." Even though the pain was becoming unbearable she replied, "No, I am not going! Our church people gave and sacrificed for this trip so I'm going to stay and enjoy this vacation! I'm going to pray and trust in God to help me." The hotel management came out to check out the accident and the very first thing she told me was, "We don't have insurance to cover anything like this." I knew that probably wasn't true but my first concern was to try to help Trish, so here I go to the drug store to pick up some medical supplies.

To spare you the difficult time she had for the next three days, let me say this; she enjoyed the sun surf even though she was in pain. We left Daytona Beach and went straight to the Urgent Care to have her wrist x-rayed. Yes, it was badly broken in two places and had to be set. Physical therapy was needed for several months, but God had another plan!

Another miracle from God was in the making! To this point, she could not pick up anything with her right hand heavier than a pencil. She had lived with much pain since the surgery for about 30 days. However, there was a Christian Ladies Retreat coming up that weekend and she felt an urge from God to attend. As the Minister of the ladies of our church, she rounded up 32 ladies and they car-pooled to the retreat. On the third day of the conference, the minister in charge suddenly called Trish out. She told her the Holy Ghost had invited her to the podium and that she was to hold up a heavy metal sword that the director had brought to the conference. She had written on the forty inch long sword the letters, "THE WORD OF GOD."

Trish immediately arose and went to the podium in faith. With her right hand she lifted up the sword unto heaven and began to speak in a heavenly language as the ladies counted to thirty-nine for the thirty-nine stripes Jesus took for our healing. The mighty power of God filled the entire congregation of over three hundred ladies. After a few minutes with Trish still holding the sword she cried out, "I am healed! I am healed! God has performed this miracle!"

The next week, we went back to her doctor as he began to remove her cast. Inside the cast he found that all the screws and plates that had been holding her bone together had worked their way out through her skin! He even had to affirm that a miracle had taken place! Until the day she passed some ten years later, she always had more strength in her right hand than her left!

MORNING STAR

"I am the Bright Morning Star." Let us stop here for a moment and if the sky is clear tonight, let's step outside and look up at the stars. Perhaps like Abraham Lincoln we'll sense that we're looking into the face of God!

Psalm 107:2, "Let the redeemed of the Lord say so, whom he hath redeemed from the hand of the enemy." If you become anxious and worried or have a "foreboding" expecting impending misfortune or evil, once you realize that the devils is trying to distract you, don't just sit around and let him beat you up with worry and negative thoughts. Open your mouth and say something he doesn't want to hear and he will leave! Begin to confess your authority in Christ! Speak the words, "Everything is going to be alright!"

Sometimes we have to do that because if we don't those evil forebodings will continue to hang around to cause us to worry with anxiety. Once you recognize anxious thoughts and evil forebodings, take authority over them and God will bring some deliverance to your life so we can begin to enjoy living.

Satan places anxious and worried thoughts in our minds, sometimes actually "bombarding" our minds with them. He hopes we will receive them and begin "saying" them out of our mouths. If we do, he then has material to actually create circumstances in our lives that he has been giving us anxious thoughts about!

Words have creative power in the spiritual realm. Genesis 1:3, God said, "Let there be...." And there was.....!

Jesus said, "Therefore take no thought saying what shall we eat or what shall we drink or wherewithal shall we be clothed?" (Matthew 6:25 paraphrase)

If we take a negative thought and start saying it, then we are only a few steps away from real problems. "Take therefore no thought for the morrow; for the morrow shall take thought for the things of itself!"

ENJOY LIFE! A gentle and peaceful spirit is not anxious or wrought up but is very precious in the sight of God. 1 Peter 3:4

Anxiety also means 'care, concern, disquietude, or a troubled state of mind'. Wrought up reflects 'tense inside'. It's like your stomach is tied up in knots and everything has become a burden to us. It causes us not to be able to relax and enjoy life as God intends. Don't be so intense. Lighten up a little. Give God a chance to work. Make the decision to enjoy life!

John 16:33, Jesus said, "I have told you these things, so that in Me you may have (perfect) peace and confidence. In the world you have tribulation and trials and distress and frustration; but be of good cheer (take courage) be confident, certain, undaunted! For I have overcome the world....!"

Philippians 4:4, the apostle Paul say, "Rejoice in the Lord always!" (delight, gladden yourselves in Him). "Again I say rejoice!"

A lady from another state wrote Trish a long letter explaining why she hadn't been healed after years of expecting to be completely healed from the illness. Here's Trish's response.

"My dear sister in Christ. You say you want someone to help you; someone who can reach the Throne of God for your healing? Well, did you know that in your letter you spoke seven times confessing your illness? There's power in the tongue and if we continually speak negative things about ourselves, be sure to know that Satan and his angels are sure to hear! They cannot do anything to you unless you speak it. You are a child of God and He wants you to be heathy and have joy and happiness.

When we start to praise Him until we really feel it and trust Him without wavering and not putting God on a timetable, "He's an on-time God!" My heart cries out to you, "Oh yes. I do know what these things are like and will go into it more later on in this letter." Speaking about God's time, sometimes ALL OF US get in His way. Yes, He could go over us, but He gave us free will, choice and speech from the beginning because of the fallen sin of man. This is not condemnation!

I had to learn about this also and He is still working on me. "You want to help?" by God's hand, I'm reading this letter from you. You will find that I can only share what I went through! You are not alone! You may think that most everyone else is fine but here am I, a cripple. You may be astonished to find that most everyone has a problem of some sort. I learned that I did not need understanding and compassion, but answers from Jehovah Nissi, my banner; my victory!

You are right about all these people you are speaking about in their illnesses. But God is touching my spirit to speak to you! STOP, STOP, watching everyone else! As you said in your own words, we are all different. Satan is using this to cause you discouragement. He wants to kill and destroy! This is spoken from God's love for you. And yes, yes, you were healed over 2000 years ago when Jesus took the stripes for our healing.

You know many people say so many things and I've sometimes thought, "You just do not know!" And the fact is, they don't. They don't know what to say or do. They want to help but we cannot focus on them. We will get nowhere. Focus your eyes on Jesus and your goal, then do whatever it takes to accomplish it. GOD WANTS TO HEAL AND BLESS US! Let's step out of his way. Remember even when it doesn't happen when you think because you are now doing something different, "IT WILL!"

You must trust and praise God for all that is not wrong; a wonderful husband, a beautiful daughter and much more. Praise Him for those things and He will prosper you with more. He loves you!

My eldest daughter is now 39. Just a couple of years ago, she lost the love of her life to death. He passed away after just seven months of marriage. But because of their coming together as husband and wife, he found Jesus Christ as his Savior for the first time in his life! Yes, sometimes it seems that we get the short end of the stick and everyone else has it better. Not always, my sweet sister! Be content in where you are in Him and just trust. He will come through for you.

This same daughter has a handicap 23 year old daughter with cerebral palsy and has always been in a wheelchair. She watched other children play, skate and do things she could not do and became very depressed. She turned to God and He is blessing her and using her to minister to others. He lets us see our afflictions and then lets us see His glory!

After reading my letter you may be thinking, "Oh no! She doesn't understand either!" Not so! I truly do! There have been so many healings and miracles in my life, I don't deserve them! Just because I've learned to understand that I am His child and He is my Father! He can fix what I cannot; but many times it has taken me a while to get out of Trish's way of thinking and out of God's way. LET GOD DO HIS WORK HIS WAY! Trust Him-He will not fail you. Yes, He gave the doctors talents, a gift, but when they can only give band-aids, He gives healing! He will amaze you, them, and everyone who saw you in your afflictions. Only God can raise you up! This builds faith, shows people the power of God and brings hope to a hopeless world. In closing, you know that creating love can be what you make it. It's really about how we love, care, and share with each other. Create new ways.....

Your friend,
Trish

Trish would eventually have the opportunity to pray with her new friend in person and the woman was miraculously healed of multiple sclerosis. To God be the glory!

CHILDREARING

Proverbs 22:6, "Train up a child in the way he should go: and when he is old he will not depart from it." Train-up has the idea of a parent graciously investing in a child whatever wisdom, love, nature and discipline is needed for him to become fully committed to God.

It presupposes the emotional and spiritual maturity of the parent to do so according to the unique personality, gifts, and aspirations of the child. It also means to train the child to avoid whatever natural tendencies he might have that would prevent total commitment to God. For example, a weak will, a lack of discipline, susceptibility to depression, etc. Hence the promise is that proper development insures the child will stay committed to God!

Let me speak about the proper discipline of children. Perhaps biblical wisdom most significantly challenges our modern philosophies and practice of child raising. Train children to honor authority, obey and to follow instructions. Discourage rebellion, stubbornness, and disobedience! Read Proverbs 13:24 and Proverbs 19:18. Practice consistent discipline and corporal correction in the rearing of children. Recognize that children are trained to obedience by these.

April 10, 2000

Living Sacrifices-Romans 12:1

Live our lives as sacrifices to God. When we do, we aren't the masters of our bodies and minds. (Also read Ephesians 4:22-24, 1 Peter 1:13-16). Worship, pray, and God will control our will, our minds, and bodies. Sacrifice your time to reach the place in relationship with Him that He is "Jehovah Shaman!" He is present! In his presence we desire to do good. This comes through diligence and sacrificial seeking daily.

In the Old Testament book of Numbers, Chapter 4:7, it speaks of "the bread of the presence." Showbread might better be interpreted as "show up bread", or in the Hebrew term, "face bread." It was a heavenly symbol of God Himself. A show up God or God's Presence shows up!

Sitting in South Carolina waiting on Nyle, studying and seeking God's face today. Lord, I am hungry for you and your presence every day in my life! I delight in your anointing! For two Sundays in a row the presence of God was so powerful. But what will we do? I feel in my spiritual nature that it's like a time bomb ready to explode, but we do not know how far to let it go. We go with it then, being so afraid of following your spirit from programs, we then continue. I'm not saying to stop preaching or stop teaching; this is necessary. But stop being time watchers, and so used to sitting down on our pews after we have experienced your presence. People are coming in hungry for your presence, they want to be filled with your Spirit; What will we do? Wait on the Lord; They will come under the supernatural moving in His presence. Help us to not be lazy or satisfied with some crumbs but with your saturated anointing!

I thank you Father, right now for your presence. Anoint me Lord! Anoint me Lord!! Let me respond to your leading and not be afraid of what others think. There are needs and people are hungry for help. Let us not send them back to their homes in a form!! What will we do?

April 15, 2000

I GOT IT!

There are many devices in a man's heart; nevertheless, the counsel of the Lord, that shall stand. God is in control. Do not bother yourself or God with questions wanting answers to every little whim! Once He does something for you and answers a need, trust in Him to take care of the details.

HOW THANKFUL ARE YOU?

One day, the father of a very wealthy family took his son on a trip to the country with the express purpose of showing him how poor people live. They spent a couple of days and nights on the farm of what would be considered a very poor family. On the return from their trip, the father asked his son, "How was the trip?" "It was great dad." "Did you see how poor people live?" the father asked. "Oh yeah", said the son. "So tell me, what did you learn from the trip?" asked the father. The son answered: "I saw that we have one dog and they had four. We have a pool that reaches to the middle of our garden and they have a creek that has no end. We have imported lanterns in our garden and they have the stars at night. Our patio reaches to the front yard and they have the whole horizon. We have a small piece of land to live on and they have fields that go beyond our sight. We have servants who serve us, but they serve others. We buy our food, but they grow theirs. We have walls around our property to protect us, they have friends to protect them." The boy's father was speechless. Then his son added, "Thanks Dad, for showing me how poor we are!"-author unknown

Isn't perspective a wonderful thing? Makes you wonder what would happen if we all gave thanks for everything we have instead of worrying about what we don't have. Appreciate everything you have, especially your friends!

REFLECT

Take a lot of time to examine yourself. When are you "most complete" and "most integrated?" Return to that place; that situation to regain the healthy sense of self that is so easily lost in our worlds clamor and activities.

DESIRE

Father, I thank you for your joy. Even though we are in the midst of sorrow, you will bring us a return of joy. My desire is to always please you and honor you with my praise. Give me that childlike faith as found in Psalms 131:1-3. In Jesus' precious Name! Amen.

John 6:23-24, "And in that day ye shall ask me nothing. Verily, verily, I say unto you, whatsoever ye ask the Father in my name, he will give it to you. Hitherto have ye asked nothing in my name, ask, and ye shall receive, that your joy be full."

4-19-2000

Verse for the day. John 16:20-22, John 16:7-24

COMING JOY

"Verily, verily, I say unto you, that ye shall weep and lament, but the world shall rejoice; and ye shall be sorrowful but your sorrow shall be turned into joy. And ye now therefore have sorrow; but I will see you again, and your heart shall rejoice and your joy no man taketh from you."

"He who goes out weeping carrying seed to sow, will return with songs of joy carrying sheaves with him." Psalms 126:6

Those words don't always start me dancing around the house, but they give me the courage to continue. Thank you, Father, that joy will follow my sorrows! The disciples were very sorrowful following the crucifixion of Jesus. Their temporary grief at the separation will be lost in the joy of a spiritual reunion!

4-20-2000

1 Corinthians 14:1

"Follow after charity (love), and desire spiritual gifts, but rather that ye may prophesy." Understand that God works through spiritual gifts to reproduce the ministry of the Lord Jesus Christ in His Church. Recognize the importance of these gifts for dynamic ministry.

"Lord, I seek your anointing in my life. Fill me with charity (love) and I desire your gifts that I may prophesy!"

4-24-2000

2 Chronicles 16:9

Do not turn away from God seeking help from others, but first and always, seek God. Maintain a heart that is fully committed to the Lord. Know that the Lord seeks out such to strengthen them and prosper their works.

The Scripture maintains a consistent testimony that those whose whole hearts are fully devoted to God are blessed by Him. Partial devotion to God or lukewarmness inevitably results in spiritual mediocrity and sporadic communion with the Lord.

"Lord, help me to always seek you daily in my life always drawing your presence near to me and trusting you for everything."

Trish preaching at our church in Oviedo, Florida in 2003

Trish at one of our children's weddings

Part II

A 75 year summary of the Life of a Preacher's Kid....
Nyle T. Vernon

The True Story of How God Completely Guided Him
Through a Life of Total Dependence on God

Nyle in 1946 Ready to Drive

In 1960 with Camper's Quartet, 2nd from left

THE EARLY YEARS

As my life was very different from Trish's life, I wanted to give you an insight into the world from my viewpoint beginning in 1944. I would not meet my beloved Trish until 1964, 20 years later. Just wanted to clarify how different each of us were and how God brought us together which resulted in 53 years of matrimony resulting in a wonderful family of three children.

Born in Radford, Virginia on July 1, 1944 to Horace Edward Vernon and my mother, Virginia Mae Vernon who rejoiced at the birth of a son. There had been a previous birth of a son two years hence, but he only lived a few months and is buried in the Radford cemetery. I remember visiting the gravesite at two years old and have a photo of a little tombstone with a little lamb carved on the top. The death of little Willie Edward would later cause my Dad to accept Christ as his Savior.

Dad was saved in a tent revival around 1946 resulting in a move to Salem, Virginia in 1947 where he gained employment at Burlington Mills in Salem. Mom began working as the State Secretary of the church of God of Prophecy in Virginia under my Grandfather, Bishop W.M. Lowman who was the State Overseer. I stayed at my grandparent's home most of the time until I started school at age six. As Mom and Dad lived just two blocks away from my grandparents, we spent a lot of time there. I was taught faith in God at an early age. My grandfather called the entire family to a time of prayer each morning before breakfast and again at night time before going to bed. In those days each prayer lasted at least thirty minutes to an hour. I thank God for the training we received at that age. It would allow me to go through life better equipped for what God had planned for us.

Back to my early memories; at the age of three, I was playing with matches in our backyard and somehow set the grass on fire and it spread to the back of our house setting it on fire! Thank God the firemen put out the fire and no one was hurt. Dad repaired the rear of the house and I never played with matches again!

Around 1949, Dad was sleeping one day as he was working third shift, and suddenly he heard his name as loud and clear as if the person was in the room with him. He jumped out of bed and looked everywhere but no one was there. He went back to sleep when the second voice called his name, "Horace!" He yelled out, "Who is there?" Once again, there was no one in the house but him. Trying to go to sleep once again, he was awakened with a clear voice which said, "Horace, go preach!" He knew it was the voice of God calling him into the ministry.

In 1950, Dad bought a nice home in Mountain View Addition, one of the first sub-divisions in that area. Grandad loaned him the money and we moved in. but there would be a testing time just a few months later. As I stated earlier, Dad was working as a night foreman at Burlington Mills. When God called him into the ministry, he resigned his job and began to pastor a church in Roanoke. After several months of struggling to make ends meet, he told my Mom he was going back to get his old job back in order to support his family. He drove to the mill and tried to turn into the parking lot as he had always had, but this time the steering wheel would not turn so he circled the block and tried the second time with the same result. God had called his name three times to go into the ministry so he decided to try one last time. Guess what? The steering wheel again refused to turn into the lot. He knew then he was being tested in his faith so he drove back home and decided to just trust God. Upon arriving, the mail had come and what do you know; there was a check for three hundred dollars. Until the day he died, he never knew who sent him that money.

A couple of weeks later, he had two women evangelists come and hold a revival at Southeast Church of God of Prophecy. It was a powerful anointed time and lasted three weeks. As he only had twenty-six members when it started, God was about to show up. At the end of the revival there was twenty-six people saved, sanctified, and received the Holy Ghost. And twenty-six newly saved people joined the church, doubling the membership!

From that time on, Dad never had to work a secular job the rest of his life! Now to a young boy I began to learn about the power of God at an early age. Whenever there was a need, I knew who to call on! The Bible says He will supply ALL of your needs.

Of course, there was always a funny side to being a preacher's kid. At the age of four, Dad was preaching one Sunday evening, when everyone began to snicker and laugh. Of course, this bothered Dad as to what was going on. Finally, he saw a little head bobbing from pew to pew, and there was little Nyle taking up an offering carrying an offering plate. Needless to say, I had collected several dollars that night. After Dad's talk to me at home that never happened again!

However, I was always looking for other opportunities. I remember back in 1950, people were getting saved every service as there seemed to be a real hunger for God. When altar time came many people would take off their jewelry and lay it on the altar as our church was very strict in those days. Well, little Nyle saw all that jewelry laying there and decided they didn't want it anymore, so I began to collect it and carry it home. My Dad began to question my newly gained wealth! Well, that soon stopped.

After the Wise Avenue location in Roanoke, Virginia, Dad would be transferred to the Norwich church also in Roanoke, Virginia. We met a lot of good people including the Vadens, Goodmans, Gillispies, Musslemans, Mitchells, and many others but cannot remember their names. Again, God blessed with His presence!

I remember it was in the Norwich church that I was first saved at about seven years of age. We were having a revival and Naman Gillispie and myself were sitting right on the front pew when conviction got ahold of us. One of us asked the other one if he wanted to go to the altar. Well, Naman got up but when I started to arise, I found I was stuck to the seat with a huge quantity of bubble gum which my Dad told me to get rid of before church. I finally got out of that mess and went to the altar where I was saved! Well, I guess that "Father knows best" after all.

It was in 1954 when I was nine years old and would be entering the fifth grade that Dad accepted a church in the country in Southwest Virginia, called Poplar Camp Church of God of Prophecy. My brothers and I were very excited about it. I remember that on the way to the new location, Dad pulled into a new car dealership in Cambria and purchased a brand, new car! We transferred all our belongings from one car to the next and completed our trip. The reason Dad wanted to trade cars before arriving at his new church was he didn't want his congregation to think he was riding in on his high horse!

Well, Poplar Camp would change my life as I have many fond memories as a boy of nine years old. I learned to hike through the mountains, to fish in the New River, and to camp out with my buddies. We had many new friends as I started school at Austinville Elementary School. Luckily, I made friends with my teacher, Mrs. Crowgey, who was the only Roman Catholic in the school and I was the only Pentecostal. We were looked at as outcasts at the time. I became the teacher's pet and made excellent grades. Guess what? She was my teacher again in the seventh grade!

I also began to mature as a Christian while at Poplar Camp. We had a strong youth department and many good people who encouraged us. Louise Frazier was my Sunday School teacher at the time. One Sunday, I offered to take the entire class to visit a cave that I had found that was close to the church. So, about ten boys and girls arrived that afternoon for the adventure. Well, I had been in the cave several times, so I would lead them (or so I thought). We crawled through the small opening into a larger room. After much squeezing through the tunnels, we finally made it to the largest room which had a deep spring of good cold water. I began to look around and could find only one girl who was brave enough to go all the way to the back of the cave, Kerry Austin. However, all six boys had made if fine.

Another time I remember that I decided to climb the large locust tree next to the driveway which was about seventy-five feet tall. I have never seen to this day a locust tree that tall. No one was home as Mom and Dad visited their members every day. Never the less, I began to climb up the tree forgetting it had sharp thorns. Oh well, what was that to a tough country boy? Everything went pretty well until I was about three fourths of the way to the top when limbs began to break as I climbed higher and higher. I finally made it just at the top when I decided it was time to back down. The only problem was, I looked down and saw how far it was to the ground and literally froze! There was no one to call for help. I remember talking to myself trying to talk me into backing down that tree. I began to descend an inch at a time expecting to fall at any second. It took me over an hour to reach the bottom and was one of the scariest times of my young life!

I also became interested in saving animals that had been abandoned by their mothers or had been injured. One day at school, one of my buddies gave me a newborn possum which had been orphaned. Little did I know, I had to be the one who fed it with a little doll bottle for it to survive. I kept it in a little cage on the back of our smokehouse until it was fully grown. One day I decided to open the door and set it free, so it could go back into the wild. The problem was that it would come out of its cage in the morning and come back to it to spend the night. However, after a month it disappeared, and I never saw it again! I also found a large dove in the ditch one day while riding my bike which had a broken wing. I gently carried it to the cage and was able to nurse it back to health. There were many other animals that had been injured that I was able to help.

When I was about twelve years old, I remember building a cabin out of small logs in Mr. Alley's woods. It was a place of my own as I began to feel like Daniel Boone or Davey Crocket who were heroes of mine. One day I went to check on my cabin when I heard something stirring around and found out it was a female bear that had given birth to two cubs the night before. Well, being twelve years old, I began to run as fast as I could towards home. The only thing was, the mother bear was right behind me thinking that I was there to do her cubs harm. I remember feeling her breath on my neck as she was that close. My Dad was standing on the back porch and said as I came out of the woods, he had never seen me run that fast! I cleared the fence around the cow pasture in one jump without slowing down. Later, several of us went back to the cabin to see if we could find the bears, but she had deserted it by that time.

As an adventuresome boy in his early teens, I loved to climb the mountain directly behind the old parsonage in which we lived. There was an old deserted house high on the mountain which was about ten miles away. Usually my friend Larry Austin and I would hike there where we would see many deer, grouse, pheasants, foxes, squirrels, rabbits and other game on our journey. But one day, on a Saturday morning, I would arise early and pack my knapsack full of sandwiches and snacks and make the journey alone. It was a beautiful day but on my return trip back home, I went down the wrong ridge and ended up getting lost! It was getting late in the evening and I was getting a little anxious about where I was. Suddenly, I saw a little dirt road ahead and decided to follow it. Guess what? It led me to a house where someone lived, and they had a telephone! I asked them where I was, and they said, "Why you're all the way into Carrol County." I had ended up in the next county. They allowed me to call my Dad who came and picked me up. It was a good lesson for me.

At this time, I didn't realize that I was building up my confidence which I would need later in life. I give a lot of credit to my Dad who had been raised up in West Virginia as a country boy. He taught me many things which would allow me to live the life of a "mountain man (or boy)." I remember that in the eighth grade at Jackson Memorial High School, I enrolled in the Agriculture class. The only problem, we didn't own a farm. One requirement was you had to have two types of livestock. Well, what could I do on only two acres of land? Finally, I decided to raise hogs and chickens. Now I didn't know anything about either, but my Dad did. We mail ordered twenty-four baby chicks and had them shipped to Alford's Store. Finally, they arrived and I brought them home to my converted chicken house to begin my life as a young farmer. With Dad's help, they grew into good layers. I believe they were called "white rock" chickens. The next thing I chose was to find two baby pigs. I was able to purchase two Hampshires from Brown Austin for twenty dollars each and having built a hog pen behind the Johnny House, I was in business! My job was to slop the hogs if you know what I mean. Well, they grew into large fat hogs and I grew fond of them giving them a name. Even though I knew we were raising them as meat for the table, it never dawned on me that in the fall of the year, it would be time to kill the hogs. I always assumed that my Dad would do that job! One cold morning in October, we got up early and built a large fire under the fifty-five-gallon barrel to boil the water as this was the way to scrape the hide from all hair and bristles. We walked to the pen and I asked my Dad, "How are you going to kill the hogs Dad?" He looked me squarely in the eye and said, "I'm not! That is your job." As I had been looking at my hogs as pets, I was not prepared for his answer. Slowly, I went into my room and picked up the 22 rifle and with two shots, it was all over. I think I became a man that day!

All my life, since I was six years old, I had wanted to be in business for myself. I wanted to be an entrepreneur! I remember I told my grandfather about my dreams and he thought I wanted to open a grocery as his father had done. He encouraged me and said maybe when I was gown he would help me to get started. At nine years old, living in the country, there wasn't many ways a kid could make money so I decided to do something on my own. Finding an old comic book where you could order greeting cards to sell, I sent in my first order and waited several weeks for them to arrive. Finally, one day, there it was! A large box had arrived full of boxes of greeting cards! I had a little red wagon and began to walk door to door selling cards. That's not an easy job in the country as the houses are so spread out. However, I managed to sell them all. This gave me courage to try another venture... Raleigh Products! Cleaning items for the home! So, I ordered a huge order with the money I had made on the greeting cards and began to sell to our family and neighbors. I was loving this selling business not knowing that at age twenty-seven that would become my career. We'll talk about that in another segment.

Through this effort at the age of nine years old, I had developed a taste for selling. I enjoyed every sale. I had begun to build up a list of repeat customers which is key to any retail business. I sold magazine subscriptions for a while that related to farming and country living but as most of my family lived in the city, I presented a sales pitch to them and every one of them bought a subscription! I realized later on in life the bought from me just to give me the confidence it took to be a salesman. Oh well! All if this happened while I lived at Poplar Camp from 1954 to 1962. In June of 1962, I graduated from Fort Chiswell High School with honors. God had certainly been good to me! Little did I know that my life was about to change drastically as we were about to move once again. Such is the life of a preacher's kid!

The Middle Years….

On July in 1962, having just graduated from high school, Dad announced that we would be moving from the country back to the city of Lynchburg, Virginia. My brothers and I were a little devastated as we were liking the country life. So on to the next appointment.

When we arrived we really did not know what to expect. I had left my friends of nine years and wondered if I would find new ones. Well, on the first Sunday at our new church, I did make two new friends that same age as me, Robert Worley and Doug Lee Cooper. As each one of us had an interest in old cars, it wasn't long before we spent our Sunday afternoons looking for antique cars that we could convert into hot rods! Worley's interest was Edsels, while Doug Lees was in Mustangs. I had not developed an interest in any particular brand at this point. Well, my next interest was to get a job if I was going to buy a car. My first out of school job was at a brand-new supermarket called the A & P. So I thought I was on my way to riches! After several months of working only thirty-two hours a week, I saved up enough money to buy my first automobile, a 1936 Plymouth coupe with a 1947 Dodge truck motor. Oh well, I thought it was a wonderful car even if it had three colors of prime! I began to think about another job with the opportunity of making more money, so I applied for three jobs the next week: GE in Salem. B&W in Lynchburg, and Mead Papermill in Lynchburg. The surprising thing was that all three of them called me to come to work the next week! It was decision time! I decided to take the Mead job as it was only about a fifteen-minute drive. To celebrate, I purchased my next car, a 1956 Buick Roadmaster convertible! She was a real beauty, yellow and white two tone. Many options were on this car, but I added one more; an under-dash record player that played six records without refilling! I truly enjoyed driving that old Buick and wish I had it today!

Well, I was learning to survive in the city life even though I still missed the mountains of Southwest Virginia. But there was a downside. As I have previously mentioned, I was saved at the age of seven. However, at the age of 18, I found myself being drawn more and more into the world. I was being influenced by others more and more. I failed God for a couple of years but God knows the future and has already planned our lives. Still working at Mead (1962-1971), I was able to purchase another one of my favorite cars. This time it was a beautiful 1962 Pontiac Bonneville convertible; burgundy with a white top and mag wheels. Boy, was I proud of that car at just 18 years old.! We had a place in Lynchburg where most every young person would cruise on Saturday night called the Southern Drive-in. A place to show off your car and of course to meet girls. But my single life had a plan that God was about to work out. On June of 1964, I was about to meet a young beautiful girl that would change my life. One day, I was waxing my Pontiac in our driveway when I noticed a young, cute girl walking towards me trying to catch her cat. I remember speaking to her and said, "Hi. What's your name?" She replied, "Patricia. My grandparents live just across the street." We talked for a while when I asked her if she would like to go out on a date sometime. She replied, "Yes, but you'll have to meet my parents first." That sounded reasonable so a couple of days later I was driving to her home. Arriving there I didn't know what to expect when her siblings began to come out one by one. Finally, her Mom and Dad came in to meet me. I did not know her dad had already told Trish to watch out for those preacher's kids! Lol! Anyway, they approved her going out with me on that first date to the drive-in theatre. We began walking toward my car when I realized all of her little brothers were following her to the car and began getting in the back seat. Her dad had told them that was the only way Patricia could go. You have to understand that I was very particular about my car. No one had ever sat in the back seat! No one had ever finger printed my chrome around the bucket seats! No one had ever placed dents in my rubber floor mats! Now I had four boys in the back seat! So off we went to the drive-in and I formulated a plan to fix the situation. I told her brothers I would give them a ten-dollar bill if they would go to the snack shack and buy popcorn and a drink and sit in front on the ground during the movie. They agreed! Problem solved. We had our privacy and they enjoyed free popcorn.

We all later became good friends as Trish would become my wife on November 21, 1964. We would remain married for 53 years when God took her home. By the way, I was wonderfully saved as I gave me heart back to the Lord at the age of twenty.

So here I am married at twenty years old and still haven't found my dream job as an entrepreneur. Where do I start? Within the first year of our marriage, Trish became pregnant with our first child. We were living in an apartment at the time, but it was time to buy our own home. Searching around, I found a home that was being foreclosed on and being sold at auction. This was close to Trish's ninth month of pregnancy. I went to the bank and found out that there was only $11,000 owed on this three-bedroom, two bath brick home and felt it was worth $40,000. Full basement and a fenced-in back yard for our child. My Dad and I drove out to visit it before the auction and decided to come to the sale. Early that morning, Trish went into labor and I had to rush her to the hospital. Good ole Dad came to the rescue and said he would go and bid for me. Well, it was snowing that morning, and no one showed up except the auctioneer, a bank official and my Dad. The auctioneer said, "we are going to have to cancel the sale because no one showed up for the sale." Dad immediately said, "I am here to place a bid for my son; he wants to buy this house. So, they took his bid of $11,000 which was the mount owed

on it. The next day, I went to the bank and signed the papers. What a miracle from God. Trish had never seen the house! Now, we had a new home to bring our new baby to! We enjoyed the house for three years and sold it for $45,000. To God be the glory! But there's a little story I want to share with you.

As I stated, my desire was to start my own business so I began to buy small antique items I could afford and set up a shop in my basement. I would run classified ads each week and started making a little money on the side. At first my wife didn't like total strangers coming into our home with a small baby around, but she learned to tolerate it. So, my first business began to grow! After a year or so, I was approached by a man who attended my Dad's church about starting a new venture together. We decided to open up an auctioning business where customers would come into our place of business and be seated while the items were being auctioned off. All brand-new merchandise. Only problem was we had no merchandise to sell. So, off we went in his covered pickup to New York City. We began to go into the smaller retail stores and ask them if they had any merchandise they would like to sell off at a discount as we were wholesalers. Believe it or not, the very first place took us up to the second floor which was a warehouse full of old brand-new items some dating back into the 1940's. We quickly filled our truck with these bargains to auction. I began to wonder who the auctioneer would be. Robert Wade, my partner, told me that would be my job. Not only was I a bit shy in front of a crowd, but I did not know how to auction. But I wanted to go into business so bad that I began to practice in front of a mirror over and over again. Finally, it was time for our weekly Saturday night auction. We had around sixty in attendance as I began to try to auction. At first my tongue got all tied up and the audience began to laugh. Boy, was I going to blow this very first attempt? So, I decided to laugh with them we had a very successful evening!

After a couple of weeks, I began to enjoy my new job while keeping my old job at Mead. On one of the buys looking for merchandise to sell, we decided to go to High Point, North Carolina and buy some furniture. I didn't know it at that time, but it would lead me into a twenty-five-year career of having my own business. We filled our truck with sofa beds and recliners to sell that next auction. Well, guess what? Not only did we sell every item, but we made more money on them than all the little items we had been selling. I began to think, why not the furniture business? Maybe that is what I want to do! To make a long story short, I sold my portion to my partner and began my journey towards my dream. At least I had $1000 for a start. With any new business, you have to raise capital. Where will it come from? Again, I went to my minister father and said, "Dad, I want to go into the furniture business. Will you give me your blessing?" He said he would pray and of course give his blessing. Man, that was all I needed to hear. As I only had limited funds, I had to figure out a way to gain more funds. Somehow, I found out that a truck dealership in Richmond, Virginia had just took in a fleet of delivery trucks with an eighteen foot body from a company and they were offering them as is for only four-hundred dollars each. So I bought me a Greyhound bus ticket and set off to Richmond. The bus only went to within ten blocks of the dealership, so I

walked the rest of the way to save money. Finally, there they were, all lined up! I picked out the one that looked pretty good and asked the salesman if they were selling them for four-hundred dollars. He told me they were, but I could only drive it around the lot. Anyway, I bought my truck and with a thirty-day tag drove it back to Lynchburg. The next day, I ran a classified ad on it for eight hundred dollars and sold it to a man who held tent revivals and needed it to move his tents around from place to place. Now I had a little more money but needed more. My brother Don, who was going to work with me got two tickets on the bus and went to Richmond once again to buy two more trucks. Selling them for eight-hundred dollars each we decided to open our first furniture store with a lot of faith. Problem was, we didn't even know where to buy our furniture.

The next venture was a very risky one and almost ended my career right there. I read in the newspaper where there was going to be a huge auction in Philadelphia, Pennsylvania of a furniture business that had been operating for over 100 years. I now had about $1600.00 to spend, so I decided to buy an airline ticket and fly to the sale. Surely, there was money to be made and we felt we were ready to fill our newly rented 2000 square foot building. My idea was to fly to the airport, get a taxi cab to the sale location, make my purchases and rent a truck and drive it back to Virginia.

The auction began, and I was high bidder on quite a number of the furniture pieces. Finally, when I had spent the entire amount of $1600.00, I went to a phone booth and began to call all the truck rental places. NO ONE HAD ANY TRUCKS TO RENT! They had all been rented to the college kids as school had just ended for summer vacation. I tried a moving and storage company who said they could deliver it to Virginia in about three months. I began to despair! Finally, I walked back to the place of auction and saw my furniture all stacked together with a sign on it that said, VERNON. Here was my furniture sitting in this building but how would I get it home? A janitor saw my distress and asked me if anything was wrong. I began to tell him I tried to rent a truck with no avail and had no way to get y furniture home. He told me to go talk to the very last truck that was loading his purchases and maybe he would help me out! Now I know that God was aware of my situation, but I also knew my Dad was praying for me. Approaching the man, I told him my story and asked him if he would consider delivering my furniture to Virginia. He said, "Yes, I am in the moving business and I am not licensed in Virginia, but this would not be the first dishonest thing I have done! "Unsure as I was about his answer, I decided to take the chance. "What would you charge me", I asked. He told me he would do it for three-hundred dollars, which I thought was very fair. I gave him the address and told him I was opening my store on the next Thursday. Flying back to Virginia, literally broke, leaving my newly purchased furniture with a stranger was of deep concern. This is where faith in God must happen. I released the newspaper ad on Monday that we were opening on Thursday even though we didn't have a piece of furniture. We waited Monday, Tuesday, no truck. No communication.

Finally, on Wednesday, the day before we were to have our grand opening, we heard a diesel truck pulling into our parking lot and there was our truck! Boy, he had come through! God was going to bless us!

Rich stepped out of the truck and said, "Vernon, you didn't have quite enough to fill the truck, so I filled out a third of it with some nice chests and dressers and bunk beds I purchased from the University of Pennsylvania. You can have them on consignment! I could not believe it as I had already spent most of my money. Pay as you sell! Rich and I later became good friends and I was able to help him many times as my business began to grow.

We opened the next day on time and by Saturday we had sold just about all the furniture. I drove to my home in my little pickup truck and ran into the house saying, "Trish, we sold out and I need some furniture to hold me over till next week. Can I take our furniture to the store? I'll buy you some better, brand-new furniture next week. So, I just about cleaned out our house. I could go on and on how much God blessed us that year as I had quit my job at Mead and was beginning my dream! One year later, we were able to purchase a nice two-acre parcel in Monroe, Virginia and would build a 16,000 square foot building as we were growing so much. God also blessed our home with two more children during this time of growth in our business. Now I had a genuine reason to succeed. God enabled us to purchase a larger home near our business as well. Finally, I had realized my childhood dream of having my very own business was coming to pass. You see, if you have a dream strong enough, and are willing to work hard, and trust in God strong enough, it will happen! NEVER GIVE UP!

We remained in the furniture business for twenty-five years and enjoyed every minute of it. My son, Troy wanted a job at six years old, so I told him I would see what I could do. The following Saturday, he rode to work with me and began his first job at fifty cents an hour. Remember, he was only six. I put him to work dusting the furniture when one of my salesmen saw him lying under a coffee table dusting the underside. He said, "Troy, what are you doing dusting that table on the underside?" Troy crawled out from under the table and replied, "My Dad said to do a good job and that's why!" Then the salesman asked him, "What's your Dad paying you?" Troy said fifty cents an hour. My salesman told him, "You should ask your Daddy for a raise!" A few minutes later I heard a knock on my office door. The door opened and there stood Troy. I said, "What do you want Troy?" He responded, "I want a raise!" I looked out through the door and all of my salesmen were laughing. I knew he had been set-up. I told him that it was the first day on the job, there would be no raise. Guess what, he quit the next day. At the age of sixteen he did go to work for me and became a very valuable employee as he went from delivery man to furniture repair man to a salesman. After a couple of years, he was promoted to assistant manager and later to manager. I guess there's value in having patience.

Over the years, I have seen how God has blessed us many times and through many decisions. I did not know where he would lead me over the next ten years of my life, but I still trusted Him!

I sold out my business in 1984 and moved to Roanoke, Virginia where my son would be attending Roanoke College. I feel today that God was getting me ready for my next calling even though I never dreamed what it would be!

Well, as we had moved we needed to find a church to attend. So many choices, but where would we end up? After visiting many churches, we found one that fit. The Pastors were Larry and Frankie Dotson who befriended us that first Sunday and even invited us to go out to dinner. Over the next thirty-five years, they became our best friends and began to nurture us in many spiritual matters. We became like real brothers and sisters! Little did I know this was a part of God's plan to begin turning our hearts in a different direction.

After moving to Roanoke, Trish began to seek the Lord for His Righteousness. At first, I thought it a passing phase, but found out later it had become her obsession! As she grew closer and closer to God it also encouraged me to do the same. As I was now working as a sales manager for a company out of Canada and traveled several days a week, Trish was able to ride with me as I had eight states to look after. She would sit in the car each time I would call on my dealers and write down in her journals what God gave to her each day. She was truly in tune with the Lord!

In 2001, God moved in a very strange way as He was about to call us into full-time ministry. Trish accepted the call first and mentioned it to me, however I was at the height of my career and did not want to give up my job. We would accept God's call to go into ministry together, but first, He showed us His Power.

One night in 2001, I awakened to find her lying on the bedroom floor at 3:13 a.m. with no sign of life in her body; no pulse, no heartbeat, no breath. She was cold and stiff. Her eyes were open, fixed and glazed. She had died! In desperation, I began to call on God to return life to her body. Praying for 35 minutes, I looked down and her little finger began to move! In just minutes she sat up and said, "Where are the angels?" GOD HAD DECIDED TO LET HER LIVE!!! It was then that I accepted God's call into the ministry as well.

Within a short time, we received a call from our dear friend who was the State Overseer of the Church of God of Prophecy in Florida, Larry Dotson. He said, "Nyle and Trish, can both of you get on separate lines; I want to ask you a question together." So, we did! The next question he asked us was, "Have you accepted a call into the ministry? The reason I asked is because I have been seeking God for Pastors for a church in Oviedo, Florida and every time I pray about it, your faces begin to flash before my eyes. Would you accept pastoring the church?" Our hearts were beating fast by this time because we knew it must be God for sure as we had spoken to no one about this. We answered back at the same time, "Yes, we accept!" What a miracle as we began a new journey!

Finally, one of God's plans for our life had been made known! Arriving at Oviedo, Florida we were excited that God would use us to be a part of His great ministry! I knew that all of my life my parents and grandparents had prayed for this day! Trish's enthusiasm became my excitement as we began our full-time ministry as Pastors. Her love for God and her faith in God was recognized right away as many people called her to pray for their needs. Many were healed and saved during our ministry at Oviedo. Glory to God! We saw the growth go from a sixteen active member church to over one hundred attending Sunday morning service. Truly, it was an amazing journey!

In 2011, at the age of seventy, I was watering my lawn one day and began to get very dizzy. I knew that something was wrong and began to back up to the front door thinking if only I can make it to inside the house it would be cool, and I would be alright. I don't know how, but I began to walk backwards one step at a time about forty steps to the door. I made it through the door but that is the last I remember that day. My daughter Renee happened to be there and said she heard someone fall and ran to see what happened. It was then she found me unconscious lying on the floor. 911 was called and I was taken to the hospital not remembering anything that was going on. The doctor told my family that I had had a brain stroke and it didn't look good and that I only had a 10% chance of surviving. My wife, who had come to the hospital in her wheelchair, looked at the doctor and said, "Doc, is there anything you can do?" He replied that I only had one vein carrying blood to my brain. There were normally five but four of those five had disintegrated. However, there was a small chance of placing a stint at the base of my brain. Trish looked at him and said, "Doc, this man has the energy of a man half his age and if you will try to save him, me and my family will sit out here and pray!" So, the doctor agreed. Five hours later, I was lying in the recovery room waiting to wake up. I remember saying, "God you have let me live. You have saved my life." You see, when I was put to sleep for the surgery I was sure I would die. But I was covered in prayer by my family! Prayer works!

In just ten days, I went home where I slept in a recliner for several days. God healed me of that stroke and there have been no problems since. However, my heart was heavy for my church. How could I properly look after my sheep with this setback? Lord, if I cannot give 100% of myself, how can I be effective as a Pastor? Trish had also begun to show signs of COPD which was affecting her breathing. We had a family meeting and decided it was time to retire at seventy years old. The State Overseer gave me a ninety-day sabbatical to make our final decision. My associate, Wes Teel, did a tremendous job looking after the church during this time and was very faithful in his position as pastor.

About the same time, my son called me one day and said, "Dad, as you know we are just completing our new home in Clermont and we want you and Mom to come and live in the in-law suite." Now I have never been in favor of children living with their parents once they are married or parents living with their children. Trish and I spent much time in prayer about the situation and decided it must be the will of the Lord, so we accepted. It turned out to be a wise move as her condition became worse and worse. I don't understand why we had to deal with these physical set-backs, but through it all we learned to trust in Jesus every day of our lives! We never gave up on His Promises! And through it all, He helped us each day.

So once again, we pulled up roots and moved to our new home in Clermont, Florida. Trish was very excited to get to decorate our two-room suite as she was an interior decorator in her earlier years. So, for a while, this gave her a distraction from her illness. We missed our many friends in Oviedo and tried to stay in touch with them as often as possible. Several things would change our lives once again. Our youngest daughter, Renee, would meet a good man from Canada and I had the privilege to marry them. Little did we imagine that she and her family would move to Canada! Trish would call her daily from her bed as by this time she wasn't able to sit up. But as a good mother does, her children would be taken care of.

Vonda, our oldest daughter was living about an hour away so we go to see her fairly often. Since we were living with our son Troy and his wife, Kathy, we felt like the family was all pulling in unity. I began attending Troy's church and was asked to be the pianist. We began to adjust to our new life. Trish had a lot of help from the health care workers who came three days a week to take care of her needs. Thank God for their help!

It was about early March in 2018 when Trish began to struggle with her breathing issue and 911 had to be called. She was admitting to South Lake Hospital where she stayed in the intensive Care Unit for 48 days! I basically moved into the hospital and spent the nights sleeping in a recliner beside her bed. As she had a tube down her throat, we couldn't communicate vocally. She tried desperately to talk, but to no avail. Finally, I was able to write on a notebook questions and she replied by writing an answer.

After 48 days, the hospital head nurse told me they were going to transfer her into another facility that specialized in helping patients who were in ICU to a regular room. So, after all this time, she was moved to Promise Hospital in The Villages which was about one hour away. At first, I tried to stay with her 24 hours a day, but it began taking its toll. I began driving home around 10:00 p.m. each night and drove back the next morning to arrive around 9:00 a.m. After fifteen additional days in the ICU, they told me they were going to remove the feeding tubes and the breathing tube obstructing her throat! O happy day! We were thrilled! Thank God for another victory!

At first, she barely could make a sound, but I was standing beside her when she said the very first audible sound. At last, my wife was making progress. She was moved to a regular room a few days later and they began to talk about her being released to go home. I went to one of the local malls and bought her a brand-new outfit for the occasion. It was a glorious week! On Thursday of that week, Trish said she wanted me to roll her to the table for dinner. It had been a year since that had happened! The entire family ate dinner that evening giving God the glory!

After that it seemed like she began to decline very rapidly as Friday and Saturday was a struggle. We prayed for God's will to be done. I tried everything I could possibly do to help her and stayed up all night to offer her comfort. At about 5:00 a.m. she began to struggle more with trying to breathe. I knew this was probably going to be her final struggle. As it was Mother's Day, I called Troy to call 911. Gently lifting her from the bed to lying on the floor, I began to do CPR according to the emergency center. This continued for about 20 minutes until the life-saving crew arrived. I knew that she had died in my arms as I moved her from the bed to the floor.

They took her to the emergency room and hooked her up to every kind of machine available. I knew in my heart that my precious little wife had already passed but stayed with her during this time. They next day, they moved her back into a room where a breathing machine kept up the sound of breathing. The entire family had gathered around her bedside at this time very distressed at the thought of losing our wife, mother, spiritual leader, and prayer warrior:

"What more could I say?"

Finally, at 3:00 p.m. the head nurse came into the room and said it was time to unhook the machine. I numbly nodded my head in agreement. A strange thing happened that I will never forget; Troy and I were standing on the right side of the bed, but her head was turned slightly to the left. After about five minutes of unhooking the machine, she turned her head to the right and looked me directly in the eye as if to say, "Don't worry. I will be alright!" I know that God did that to give me comfort. They pronounced her dead at 3:05 p.m.

We managed to have her funeral in Oviedo where our former Pastor, Tim Coalter, had flown in from Cleveland, Tennessee to preach her service which had been her request. Our family is indebted to him to this day!

Over the next few weeks and months, I began to sink into a deep depression for the first time in my life. Many times, in our ministry, we tried to help people in a depressed state, never had I imagined what it really felt like! I sat in the recliner and just waited to die! I felt like I had nothing to life for! About two weeks after Trish's death, I had a severe pain that went through my heart and I felt like I was dying. Troy immediately got me to the hospital even though I don't remember anything. I was transferred to the Orlando Regional Hospital where the Heart Specialist said I had five blockages in my heart and would need immediate surgery. Once again, I was at the mercies of God! I knew my family would be praying for me, so I was put to sleep but not before praying the 23rd Psalm. I was not expecting to come out alive for this procedure.

Through the mercies of God, I did survive. I remember that when I was trying to awake in the recovery room, I could not yet open my eyes, but I said to God, "God am I in heaven?" Finally, my eyes opened up and I began looking around and saw all of the patients there in the recovery room and knew this wasn't heaven!

I had an experience in the hospital that I would like to relate to you. Never in my life, have I taken drugs for anything except once for pain for a kidney stone many years ago. However, the doctor gave me something I will never forget. I began hallucinating with visions and nightmares that were real to me at that time! I won't tell you all the details, but they were so genuine and so real that I believed them. Troy came to see me, and I told him they had moved me to a different place that was horrifying! He tried to reassure me that I was in the same hospital, but my mind just wouldn't accept it. This went on for several days of unbelievable agony!

Finally, because of my insistence of asking my doctor to allow me to go home after eight days, he final agreed under certain conditions! So, I checked out of the hospital and went home to recover. The first few nights, I had to sleep in my recliner due to the pain. Troy and Kathy would stay with me to make sure I was alright. Many people were praying for my recovery and I could feel their prayers!

As the days begin to drag into weeks, my depression was once again trying to take over my life. Even though my trust in God never wavered, I did not look forward to awakening to another day. There was just an emptiness within my heart. If you have never lost a companion, you probably cannot relate to this, but believe me, it is a real feeling!

I remained in that posture for the next several months as we were now into the fall of 2018. My children were aware of my state of mind and were concerned. But something would change that would once again renew my life! IT IS CALLED HOPE! Now I have always heard that a drowning man will reach for a straw even if he is about to drown in the ocean. Reaching for the straw renews hope!

Around December of 2018, my son announced to me that they wanted to take me to Virginia for Christmas to see my brothers and other family. I agreed to this as I really needed a change. Little did I know a big change was about to happen that I never imagined. We made the eleven-hour journey and stayed in a nice little rental house. The next day, we began to reconnect with all of our family. For several months, God had been urging me to contact my late wife's family wherever they were and tell them I loved them. I began to find them one by one and did what I felt like God had instructed me to do. The first stop would be the home of Tommy and Valerie Brooks who are my niece and her husband. All of the family were there when we arrived. As I had not seen many of them in years, it was quite a homecoming day!

My former sister-in-law, Deloris and I began to talk as her husband had passed away about five years earlier. We began to find much to talk about and spent the entire day reconnecting.

The next day, we met with my side of the family, Don and Gary, my brothers, as well as, their wives and children. It was indeed a very good trip! I felt encouraged and excited. After a few days, it was time to make the journey back to Florida, but our friendship would remain strong. Arriving home, I began to send Facebook messages to Deloris and we began to talk on the phone each evening and related old times. Her encouragement and prayers for me were a godsend! Over the weeks and months that followed we realized that our love was beginning to flourish.

Now, as we both are Christians, we spent much time in prayer as we both had loved our deceased companions dearly and we wanted God's favor in this. None of us knows what the future holds but we know who holds the future! It has been 1 ½ years since the day we reconnected and now are engaged to be married in the near future! We serve an Awesome God!

As the final chapter of this book, I wanted to leave you with these thoughts. No matter how far you have fallen, never give up hope! It's kind of like faith, it's something you can see in your mind and feel in your spirit, and you believe that it will happen!

For 75 years, I have to say that God has kept me and blessed me abundantly. He has given to me a wonderful family who are serving Him. He has placed many people in my life who would mentor me to walk in paths of righteousness! I am not perfect, but I am striving for it. With His help, I plan to make my journey home someday. If he allows me to live, I will serve Him with great indebtedness. As I now look into the heavens in the beautiful skies of Florida, I now have great peace! My prayer is that this book will bless you in some way as it shows the magnificence of how God directs our life to serve Him.

The Future...

Who knows? At 75 years old at this writing, I realize that a man cannot live forever. We are all at the mercies of God! We are aware of His soon coming so we must remain ready. 1 Thessalonians 4:16-17 says, "For the Lord

Himself will come down from heaven with a loud command, with the voice of the archangel and with the trumpet call of God, and the dead in Christ will rise first. After that, we who are still alive and are left will be caught up together with them in the clouds to meet the Lord in the air!"

I am looking forward to seeing my many family members who have already gone and my friends who encouraged me. But I really want to see Jesus, the one who died on the cross for my sins! I want to worship around the throne of God in gratefulness!

So what do I see in my future on earth? Number 1, I want to live a peaceful life. Number 2, I want to be a blessing to others. Number 3, I want to serve God to the fullest and remain a minister the rest of my life. Whatever God wants me to do, I never wish to say no whether it is preaching, singing, playing music, or just being a one on one witness for Him! We are living in a world that needs someone to show them they are loved! So many families have to work two jobs to keep up and have very little time to raise their children properly. Children will imitate what they have seen and heard. If there is constant arguing in the home, that will probably follow their lives. If there is a Christian upbringing in their lives, then they will wish to follow a life of blessings. There are some things even the most wonderful school teacher cannot teach them.

What are some of the values that I find important in my own life? Well, I have learned that the love for money will not satisfy our desires but only for a short while. While it is important we need to work for whatever we need, spending time with those we love will supersede riches. Long after they are grown, our children will remember the small things much better than the larger things.

On a personal level, I still love to travel this beautiful country that God has allowed us to live in. The mountains, the oceans, and all the animals are all living in harmony with nature. If mankind could only learn from that, what a wonderful world it would be! The Bible tells us to "love our neighbor as thyself!" When I was a child, we knew every neighbor on our block. Now we don't even know our next-door neighbor's name or where they are from. It even tells us in Matthew 5:44, "But I say unto you, love your enemies, bless them that curse you, do good to them that hate you, and pray for them which despitefully use you, and persecute you." Now, I will admit that it is very hard to love enemies and I have had to deal with it many times. But I found that if I did good for evil, it would cause things to turn around. The enemy is full of hate but as Christians we cannot fight fire with fire! We must fight on our knees in prayer!

In my future, I see a life that is bright and not dim. We can speak either blessings or curses on our life, and I'm going to speak blessings! There is a good possibility that I will move back to my home state of Virginia. I have had a good life in Florida for the past 20 years and there are no regrets. There has come a time in my life that I am missing the mountains that I once called home! There are old friends that are still faithful and I would like to sit down with them and talk about the "good ole day!" Whatever God has left for me, I want to be a willing servant. Thank you for letting me share my thoughts with you!

PART III

The Next Generation

How God's Blessings continue to flow to the children.

Vonda, Troy and Renee together

There's a scripture in the Bible that says, "Train up a child in the way he should go: and when he is old, he will not depart from it." (Proverbs 22:6) We have always tried to practice this teaching with raising our children. Whenever I was out of town on a business trip, Trish would take the kids to church three times a week. Guess what? They are still going to church and now raising their own children to serve the Lord!

Our very first child was born in 1965 and we were blessed with a healthy child who favored her Mom with brown eyes and dark hair. Everyone at my Dad's church wanted to spoil her as well as her grandparents. We named her Vonda Kay after the 1965 Miss America! We had a great life going to the beach at Long Beach, North Carolina. She helped her mother quite a bit in raising the other two siblings when they arrived, being the eldest. After her marriage, God blessed her with three children, Brandi, Cortney and Jonathan. She later moved to Florida.

I would like to fast forward to the year 2006 while Trish and I were pastors at the Oviedo Church of God of Prophecy. God blessed us with a powerful spirit-filled service one Sunday evening and several who were in attendance were healed. No one knew but Trish and I that Vonda had just received word from her doctor that she had an inoperable brain tumor! This was devastating news to us as well as to her. But our faith in God remained, for with God all things are possible. That very night, she was miraculously healed!! What a great time as we worshipped God that night! Returning back to her doctor for a follow-up visit, he was very surprised to find no tumor! It had completely gone away! Glory be to our Savior! She had been completely healed!!! She is presently living in Deltona, Florida where she works as a veterinarian assistant. She has been a widow for the past two years after her husband Joe passed away. But praise God, she is attending the Sanford Church of God of Prophecy and serving the Lord.

God blessed us with a second child in 1968, a son whom we named Troy Thomas. He was a very good boy and obedient to his parents. I was able to bring him a little puppy home one day when he was around seven years old that he named "Old Yeller!" That dog protected him twenty-four hours a day. His favorite riding toy was the "Green Machine" that he treasured. Trish and I felt like God had His hand upon his life at an early age and would use him in the ministry some day. His interest in serving God was a big factor in his life as he volunteered for youth mission teams and youth camps at an early age. Thank God, for years later this training would pay off. He began to attend Roanoke College after graduating high school and received his degree. Things went smooth for several years, but little did we know that he would face one of the biggest obstacles of his life. At age 25, he was diagnosed with a terrible disease called muscular dystrophy. We could hardly believe it! Still single, he was facing a real dilemma. We took Troy to the best doctors at LewisGale Medical Center, the UNC Medical Center, as well as, Duke University Hospital where he met Dr. Tims. After multiple examinations and tests, Troy received his diagnosis...muscular dystrophy. The doctor was expecting them to break out in tears, but Trish and Troy only smiled. He said, "Did you hear what I said? You don't seem to be upset!" But they only smiled. They told him, "You see, people are already praying for his healing even though they do not know what's wrong." When they walked out of that office, Troy and his mom looked at each other and Troy said, "Do you feel what I feel?" She said, "Yes, God is going to heal you."

One summer night in 1995, around 3:00 a.m. I received a phone call from Troy asking me if I could come to his house immediately. Living only three miles away, I made the trip in about ten minutes. I don't know how I was able to go through the locked front door but went straight into his bedroom where he was sitting on the side of the bed in turmoil. He said it was as if the devil himself was attacking his mind. He was desperate and afraid. I went to battle in prayer on Troy's behalf, praying until the enemy left and we won the victory! After that, Troy was able to go right to sleep.

One Sunday morning in late January of 1996, Troy was leading praise and worship for what he thought would be his last time. As he was very weak at the time he could barely hold the microphone to his mouth with both hands. I remember the song we were singing that day, "Victory in Jesus!" He led the second verse, "I heard about His healing, of His cleansing power revealing, how He made the lame to walk again and caused the blind to see!"

Suddenly he handed the microphone to one of the choir members and began to run around the church. Needless to say, the entire church began to shout praises to God for they had indeed seen a real miracle! The second time around, I joined him in his praise run. What a tremendous service that day for this was truly a great miracle of God! Troy later shared that as he was singing the verse, he heard God say "RUN!" He said that with every lap he began to get stronger and stronger until he couldn't run anymore and fell flat on his face laughing and crying.

Later that week, Troy would meet his future wife, Kathy. They followed Trish and I to Florida in 2003. At first, he worked at several good jobs, but just couldn't find his place it seemed. One day, he was driving past the State Office of the Florida Church of God of Prophecy in Winter Garden when God instructed him to pull into the parking lot. Obeying God, he pulled in and parked. This happened on several occasions. Every time he parked there a feeling of peace came over him. On one occasion, he felt compelled to go in and say hello to the new State Overseer and his wife, Bishop Robert and Maryann Davis. After sharing with Maryann about his life and how he never quite felt like he had found his place she said, "Troy, you need to talk to Bob." At the end of the conversation she looked him right in the eye and said, "Just say 'yes' and see what God does!" Troy walked to his car, praying "I don't know what this means, but it's a 'yes'". Well, to make a long story short, he now knew why he had moved to Florida. He has worked as the State Treasurer for many years as well as the State Prayer Coordinator. In October of 2010, he was appointed as pastor of the Leesburg Church of God of Prophecy where he has served for ten years! He had finally found his place where God wanted him to be. Now he is able to share personally how he was healed of muscular dystrophy everywhere he goes! What a great testimony of God's great power!

In 1969, we would be blessed once again with a new baby girl named Tammy Renee who turned out to be a real joy in our lives. She was a happy-go-lucky type of child and being the baby of the family, she was perhaps a little spoiled. She followed the other two siblings in her desire to attend church and follow Jesus Christ as her Lord and Savior. After completing high school, she was offered a career job by Sam Walton, the founder of the big box store called Sam's Club. Along with her girlfriend, they would work a dream job directly under Sam Walton as they traveled all over the east coast obtaining memberships for the Club. They were paid well as she sent her checks home to Trish to deposit for her. She would marry within a few years and would end her career at Sam's. You see, God has a reason for everything if you trust Him! She had two sons, Trevor and Caleb. She also adopted a little boy named Scotty at the age of six. Then, about eight years ago, she adopted a beautiful little girl named Ariana who has been a blessing everywhere she goes. Her husband, Devlin and Renee are pastoring a church in Camden Ontario, Canada! She has been healed many times by God's power and remains a strong prayer warrior to this day! We have truly been blessed! I praise God for His continued favor upon our children. Even though I cannot visit with them often, I know that God is with them and is using them in His ministry to help others. Praise His Holy Name!

In the closing of this chapter, our family has adopted a wonderful old church hymn as our battle cry. Here are the words:

Sing the wonderous love of Jesus
Sing his mercies and his grace
In the mansions bright and blessed
He'll prepare for us a place.

When we all get to heaven
What a day of rejoicing that will be
When we all see Jesus
We'll sing and shout the victory!

Nyle & Trish at the church they pastored for 14 years in Oviedo.
2001-2014

FL Sunset

Printed in the United States
By Bookmasters